ACROPOLIS MUSEUM
ATHENS

BERNARD TSCHUMI

ACROPOLIS MUSEUM
ATHENS

Photographic essay by Peter Mauss

Ediciones Polígrafa

© of this edition: Ediciones Polígrafa, Barcelona, 2010
Balmes, 54. 08007 Barcelona (Spain)
www.edicionespoligrafa.com

© of the photographs, texts, and translations: the authors

Photographic credits: Nikos Daniilidis (pp. 7, 30); Christian Richters (pp. 10-11);
Peter Mauss / Esto (pp. 34-71)

Concept of the Collection: Francisco Rei
Coordination: Marcela Carrasquilla
Copy Editor: Richard G. Gallin
Design: mot (www.motstudio.com)
Page layout: Estudi Polígrafa / Carlos J. Santos
Color separation: Estudi Polígrafa / Annel Biu
Printing and binding: Novoprint, Barcelona (Spain)

Available in USA and Canada through D.A.P./Distributed Art Publishers
155 Sixth Avenue, 2nd Floor, New York, N.Y. 10013
Tel. (212) 627-1999; Fax: (212) 627-9484

ISBN: 978-84-343-1234-0
Dep. legal: B. 27.173 - 2010

CONTENTS

Foreword
Dimitrios Pandermalis
8-9

"We wanted the
museum to achieve a
kind of timelessness"
Conversation with
Bernard Tschumi
13-31

Photographic Essay
Peter Mauss
33-71

Project Memory
72-75

Project Data
76-77

Select Bibliography
78-79

Aerial view of
the Acropolis Museum
and surrounding area,
Athens, Greece
Photo: Nikos Daniilidis

(pages 10-11)
Outside view of the
Museum looking at
the entrance canopy
Photo: Christian Richters

An extended archaeological excavation undertaken over seven years on the site of the new Acropolis Museum revealed the remains of a neighborhood from the ancient city of Athens. The result: a new life-size exhibit for the Museum had come to light. The over 4,000 square meters of ancient ruins dictated the final orientation of the new Acropolis Museum and the shape of the Museum at its base. Over a period of months, archaeologists and architects carefully examined the excavation in order to be able to locate the building's foundation piles without damage to the ruins, resulting in an interesting juxtaposition of new technology and ancient constructions. For visitors who will eventually be able to walk through the ancient neighborhood below the Museum building, the dramatic difference between the building's solid concrete-and-glass construction and the fragile ancient walls works well in enabling visitors to recognize two different yet coexisting worlds. Daylight reaches the excavation both from openings in the perimetric walls of the archaeological site and through the huge glass windows that are inlaid in the ground floor of the Museum. These create an atmospheric experience within the excavation and an additional surprise for visitors who enter the Museum on the ground floor and have unexpected and panoramic views of the excavation below.

Entering the Museum lobby, visitors are able to view a powerful rectangular concrete core surrounded by large cement columns that recall the architecture of an ancient temple. The core, with precisely the same dimensions and orientation as the cella of the Parthenon, rises through the building to its third and final floor where it becomes the mount for the 160-meter-long frieze of the Parthenon. A basic principle underlying the Museum's design was not to imitate the architecture of the ancient monuments but to make silent reference to them. The cement core provides the capacity to exhibit the famous frieze in precisely the same order and sequence as when it adorned the monument, and the cement core directly influenced the structural, architectural, and aesthetic form of the building.

It is not accidental that the first exhibition space—a long ascending hall on the ground floor—draws on the ascending pathway to the Acropolis monuments: the symbolic rise of the Gallery of the Slopes alludes directly to the climb to the hilltop of the Acropolis. Statues, inscriptions, and ceramics derived from the sanctuaries and residences that once were found on the slopes of the Acropolis are displayed on the glass ramp of this gallery.

The south wing of the first floor displays the famous finds from the sixth-century BC Acropolis that represent aristocratic Athens. Two key elements characterize the Archaic Gallery: first, the tall cement columns that allude to the architecture of sacred environments, and, second, the abundance of natural light that enters the Gallery from the fifty skylights above and from the vast glass wall on the south side of the building. Natural light is regulated by the fritted glass and the black shades. Consideration of their optimum exhibition in relation to the natural light determined the final positioning of the individual exhibits. Directly above, on the third floor, is the culmination of the Museum's exhibition, the Gallery of the Parthenon of the Classical era with the sculptures of the emblematic monument—the Temple of Athena Parthenos.

Inside the central core of the building, on a first-floor balcony that overlooks both the Gallery of the Slopes of the Acropolis and the excavation beneath the building, stands one of the most prominent groups of statues from the Acropolis, the Caryatids of the Erechtheion. Visitors can view these elegant sculptures and enjoy their beauty for the first time at close proximity. The Caryatids can also be seen from a distance both from a first-floor landing and from second-floor balconies, hence enabling visitors to appreciate their beauty as individual statues and as architectural members.

The top of the Museum building, a glass encased boxlike structure, was designed with the needs of the exhibition program. At this level, the Parthenon Frieze not only wraps around the cement core, but forty-six stainless-steel columns that replicate the number and spacing of the columns of the Parthenon, surround the core and provide the framework for the mounting of the metopes of the Parthenon. At the front and the rear of the Parthenon Gallery, the surviving pediment sculptures are presented. For the first time in modern history all the surviving sculptural fragments of the Parthenon are reunited and provide the most complete picture of the original temple. Unfortunately, a good part of these are cast copies, as the originals remain in the British Museum.

The new Acropolis Museum is a site-specific museum. After a daring decision the building was dressed with glass facades that allow direct dialogue between the archaeological site to which it refers and the modern city in which it is located. The Museum confidently does not hesitate to invite both historic and contemporary Athens with its picturesque hills and its chaotic modernity into the Museum, differentiating it from the majority of traditional archaeological museums today. The Acropolis Museum is admirable evidence of the outcome of an excellent working relationship between curator and architect.

Dimitrios Pandermalis
President
Acropolis Museum

"WE WANTED
THE MUSEUM TO
ACHIEVE A KIND
OF TIMELESSNESS"

Conversation with
Bernard Tschumi

Question_ As in any creative field, architects must reconcile their background and experience with the cultural reality of their time. Would you tell us about your training?

Bernard Tschumi_ The study of architecture and my pragmatic experience in construction have been essential to my training, but just as important are literature and other cultural fields. Architecture eventually became the common denominator for all of those experiences.

What literary aspects (novels, poetry, philosophy) would you stress?

The range is really large. Anything from a short detective story by Edgar Allan Poe to the complete works of James Joyce.

As distinct from other typologies, the architectural conception of a museum must take into account the critical presence of the artwork. Do you regard this dialectical confrontation between the two practices as an added difficulty?

In the case of the new Acropolis Museum, we had the advantage of knowing ahead of time each of the pieces that would go into the Museum. Rather than a dialectical confrontation, we saw it as a particular type of complementarity, whereby the following major issues had to be addressed: the use of daylight, the use of soft sanded concrete to act as a background to the sculptures (the concrete absorbs the light and the marble sculptures reflect it), and last but not least the relation between the artworks and the movement sequence among them.

What has been your approach to art?

Art is very different from architecture; sometimes they share a similar approach. But, the approach to making contemporary art is very different from what we did at the new Acropolis Museum. We really took a long-term view. We wanted the Museum to achieve a kind of timelessness.

But as far as your personal training is concerned, regardless of your recent experience at the new Acropolis Museum, how important was art?

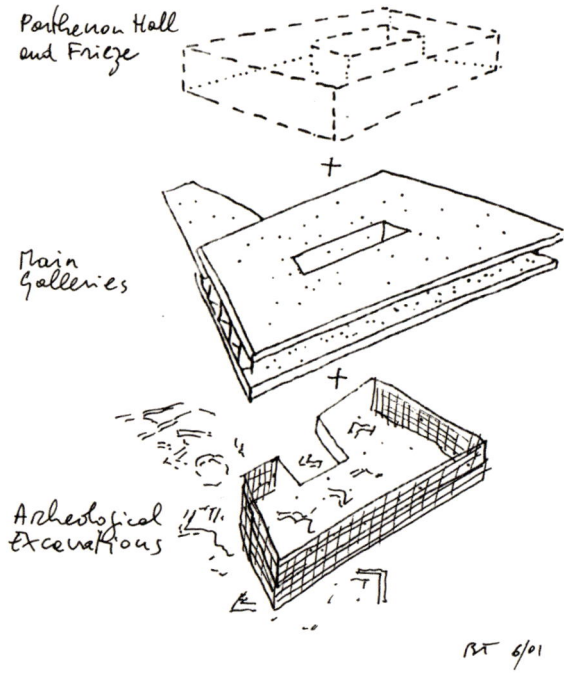

Parthenon Hall and Frieze

Main Galleries

Archeological Excavations

BT 6/01

Bernard Tschumi
Acropolis Museum,
exploded axonometric sketch

Much of the twentieth-century avant-garde, as well as Conceptual and performance art, certainly had much influence on my early work.

And in the field of architecture, what have been your referents?

We see architecture as a dynamic environment, where what happens in a space is as important as the space itself; hence, my interest in ideas of montage, sequence, notation. Film theory was a starting point in the early days of my work and informed some of my interest in the importance of program.

In this editing and quotation process, what images from the history of architecture come to your mind?

Too many architectural images come to mind—the list of antecedents is always large. But I'll just mention one, quoted by Sergei Eisenstein, the early revolutionary Russian filmmaker, who in his famous text "Architecture and Montage" shows a plan from a book by the historian Auguste Choisy and says it is the origin of cinema. And what is the plan? The Acropolis.

In a recent interview you said that the new Acropolis Museum was an exception among your projects. What are the aspects that you consider to lay outside of your usual architectural practice?

Never before had the context played such a strong role as at the new Acropolis Museum. We used to emphasize concept and content until then. The design of the museum was entirely shaped by the context, both architectural, urbanistic, and cultural to such a degree that we went back and looked at how this had been at work in other projects.

You have also spoken of your understanding of architectural production as analogous to mathematics—the stating of a hypothesis and its demonstration through the work. How would you define the notion of concept in architecture?

Starting with a concept or an idea is different from starting from form or function. A concept is an overriding idea, diagram, or scheme that gives coherence and identity to a building. Concept, not form, is what distinguishes architecture from mere building.

Continuing with analogies, in this case contextual, when seen from above, the Museum —like a hill—appears to be crowned by a top floor that re-creates the scale of the Parthenon. What other analogous elements can we find here?

You have to read the Museum as the superimposition of three autonomous volumes: the lower one addresses the archaeological excavation, the middle one is oriented according to the surrounding street grid and houses mostly the Archaic collection of sculptures, and the top one addresses the Parthenon and is oriented parallel to it. It houses the famous Parthenon Frieze. It is possible to read the sequence of these spaces as analogous to ascending the Acropolis, but there is also a reading of ascending through layers of history that is just as valid.

The uppermost volume of the building seems to rotate in order to adopt the orientation of the Parthenon, but we find no hint of color on its surface, although we know that the original was polychrome. We also know how skillfully you make use of color (Florida International University's Paul L. Cejas School of Architecture Building, 1999–2003). Is this an exercise in neutrality or is there an appreciation here of the archaeological datum over the historical discourse?

Much of our concept for the Museum is about the natural light. We deliberately tried to avoid any trace of artificial color in the light for the sculptures. Indeed, we spent a lot of time making sure the glass would be extra-pure, so as to avoid its usual greenish tint. Each project has its own logic; we use color only when it reinforces the concept.

After the Second World War, museum architecture took a markedly iconic turn (Wright, Niemeyer...) which seems to be accentuated in the latest generation of museums. Where would you situate your own experience?

I feel quite reticent toward the idea of form for form's sake. What counts is that architectural form must be as much about what it does as about what it looks like. (Hence, I like Wright's Guggenheim very much, as the concept of the ramp as movement through artworks is evident throughout the design.)

In a museum the light is obviously very important. To what extent has the proposed treatment affected the form of the building?

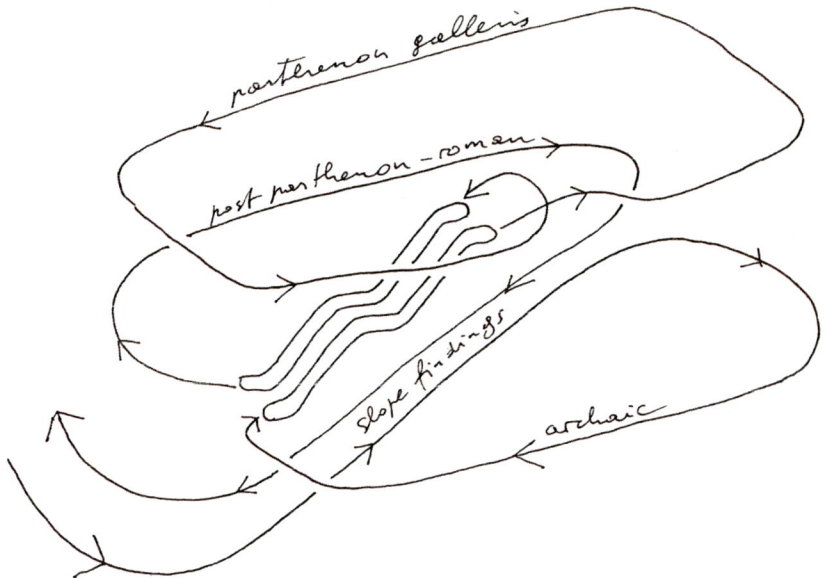

parterenon galleris

post parthenon – romen

slope findings

archaic

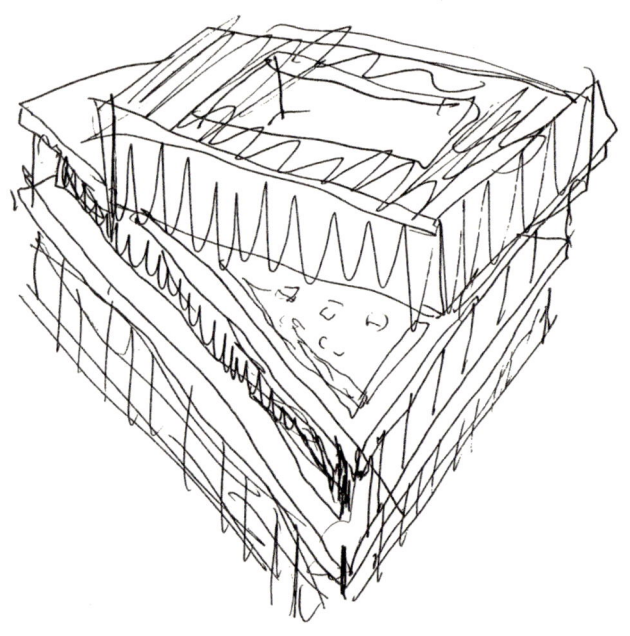

Bernard Tschumi
Volume sketch
of the building

(page 21) Site plan
and section in relation
to the Acropolis

Enormously so, in two cases in particular: first the Archaic Gallery with its skylights that give an unusually natural light to the sculptures, and second, the Parthenon Gallery where the pediments and frieze had to be oriented exactly like the Parthenon itself. The way the glass is used is directly a function of the light.

What particular features of the proposed circulation plan should we focus on?

In an important diagram, we show how the building works as a loop, starting with the glass ramp over the excavations, meandering through the statues and the columns of the Archaic Gallery, and finally walking along the narrative of the Parthenon Frieze before returning through the later, Roman era galleries.

And the museological program: to what extent has it determined the project?

The museological program by Professor Dimitrios Pandermalis and our architectural concept were purposefully made to coincide exactly not only at the stage of the competition for the building but also during the several years of construction, thanks to an unusually close collaboration between curators and architects.

In the last decade we have also found you reflecting on what could be thought of as a rereading of your experience in terms of the binomial concept and/or context.

Yes, indeed. We started to look at our earlier projects and realized that the triad concept, content, and context has always been important for us. Reading architecture is not static; it is often helpful to look at previous work as it may relate to your current ideas.

The importance of context has become a commonplace in architectural thinking in recent decades. In this light, what are the conceptual elements—of style, of scale and so forth—that have been present in the genesis of the project?

I do not mean context in terms of the common sense of "contextualism," which I intensely dislike. Our approach to context is to cultivate reciprocity, indifference, or conflict, depending on the circumstances.

In the case of the new Acropolis Museum, how should we approach the strategies of reciprocity, indifference, and conflict that you apply to both the program and the context?

Mostly through what we call *reciprocity*—for example, with the large glass rectangular gallery at the top of the Museum in dialogue with the Parthenon. While most people understood and appreciated that strategy, some people felt that it was a conflict and out of character. I feel we were right.

The German artist Blinky Palermo referred to the architectural spaces in which he intervened as *objets trouvés*. I seem to recall your referring to the context—in the sense of space—in the same terms.

You can say that the archaeological remnants below the Museum were our *objets trouvés*.

Until very recently, the museum was regarded as a space for reflection and contemplation, the locus of aesthetic experience—with all of the mystical resonances that might be ascribed to it. Now, however, it forms part of a dynamic of consumption, which the architecture must obviously take into consideration.

Yes.

Mechanical stairs, gift shops, cafeterias… all of them are elements that new museological programs must cover and take into account. What relevance do you confer upon them?

At the new Acropolis Museum, we tried to make them secondary to the art. But I am aware that in some other museums, they have increasingly become part of the experience.

In recent architectural vocabulary the most frequently used terms—and the ones that largely determine the modus operandi of the present moment—refer to *folds*, *layers* and *displacements*. Do you believe we really have gained in organicism, transparency, and adaptability, as these concepts seem to suggest?

Words are important, as they help to qualify certain ideas. But they should not be taken too literally: a folded wall has very little to do with Gilles Deleuze's theory of the fold (as in his *The Fold: Leibniz and the Baroque*), for example.

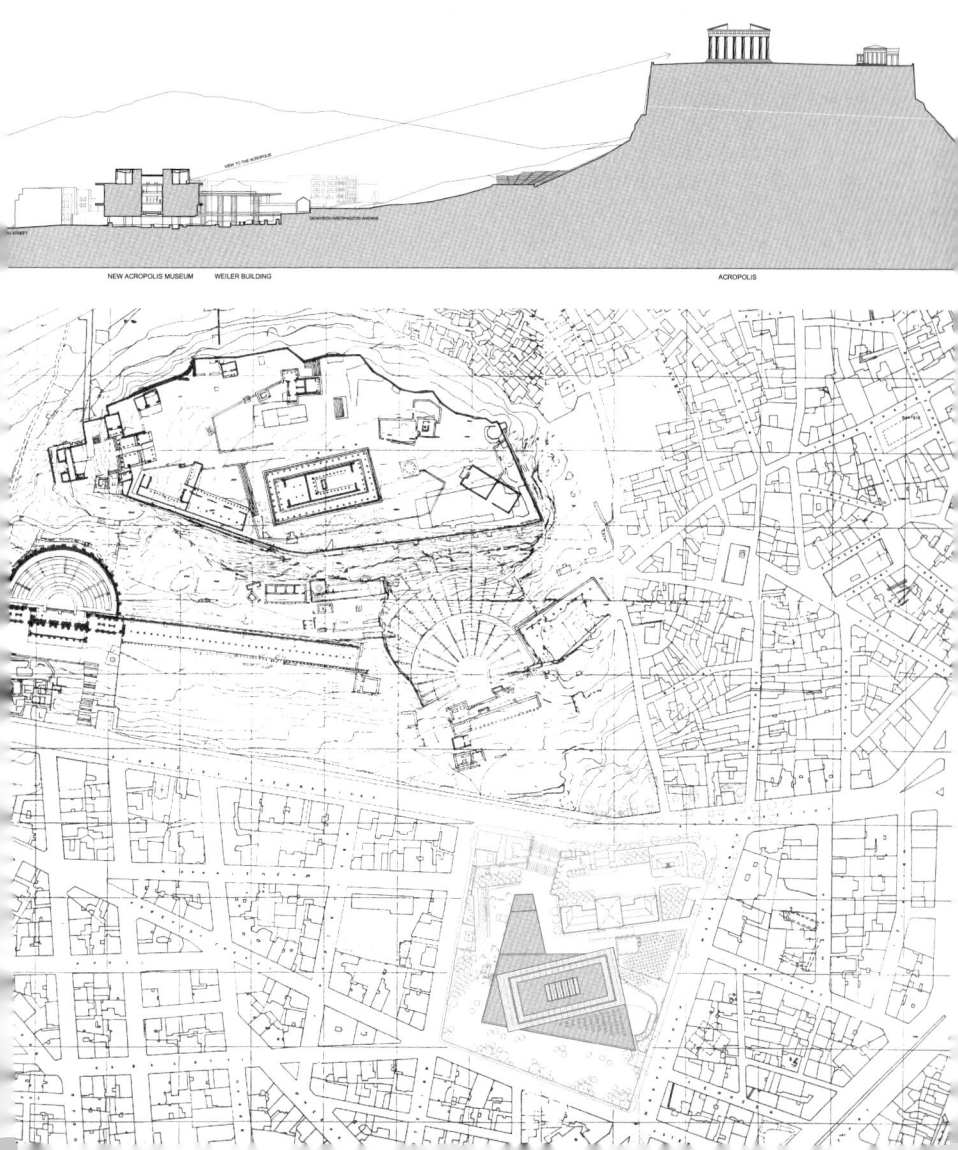

NEW ACROPOLIS MUSEUM   WEILER BUILDING   ACROPOLIS

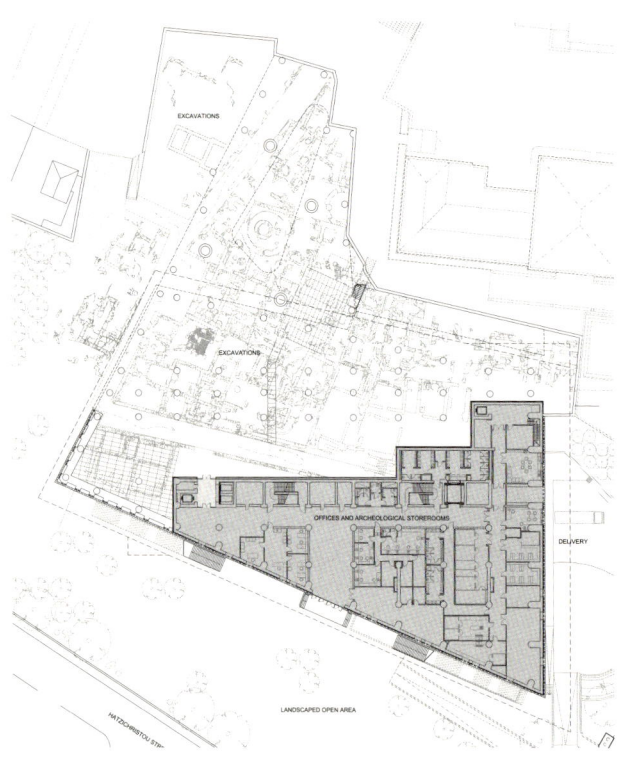

EXCAVATIONS

EXCAVATIONS

OFFICES AND ARCHEOLOGICAL STOREROOMS

DELIVERY

LANDSCAPED OPEN AREA

HATZICHRISTOU STR.

0   2,5 5   10   20

meters

N

Floor plan of level −1

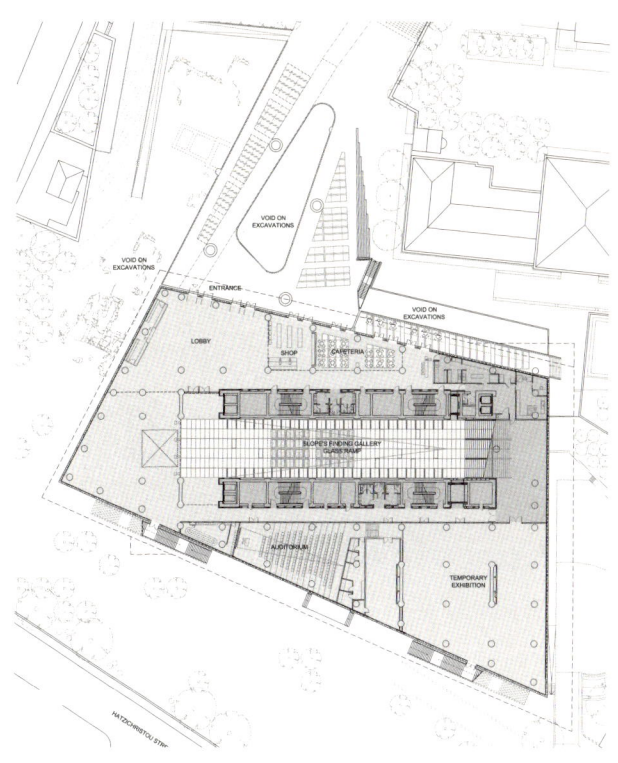

VOID ON
EXCAVATIONS

VOID ON
EXCAVATIONS

ENTRANCE

VOID ON
EXCAVATIONS

LOBBY

SHOP

CAFETERIA

SLOPE'S FINDING GALLERY
GLASS RAMP

AUDITORIUM

TEMPORARY
EXHIBITION

HATZICHRISTOU STR.

Floor plan of level +0

0   2,5 5   10   20

meters

N

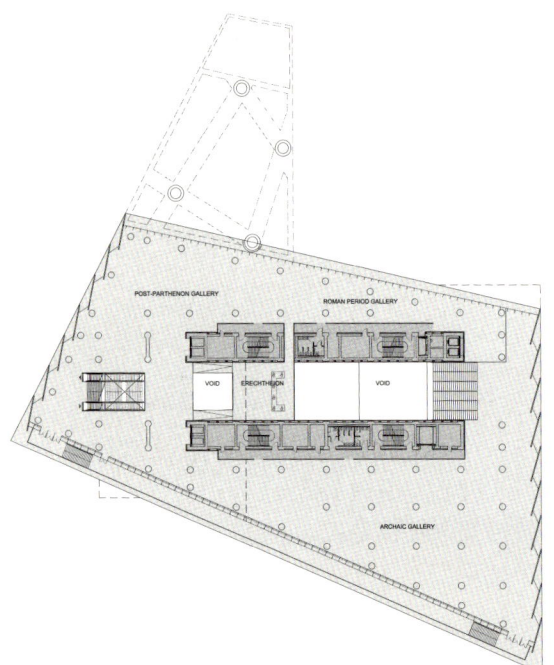

POST-PARTHENON GALLERY

ROMAN PERIOD GALLERY

VOID

ERECHTHEION

VOID

ARCHAIC GALLERY

0   2,5 5   10   20

meters

N

Floor plan of level +2

PUBLIC
TERRACE

SHOP

RESTAURANT

LOUNGE

VOID

BALCONY
LOUNGE

VOID

0   2,5 5   10   20

meters

N

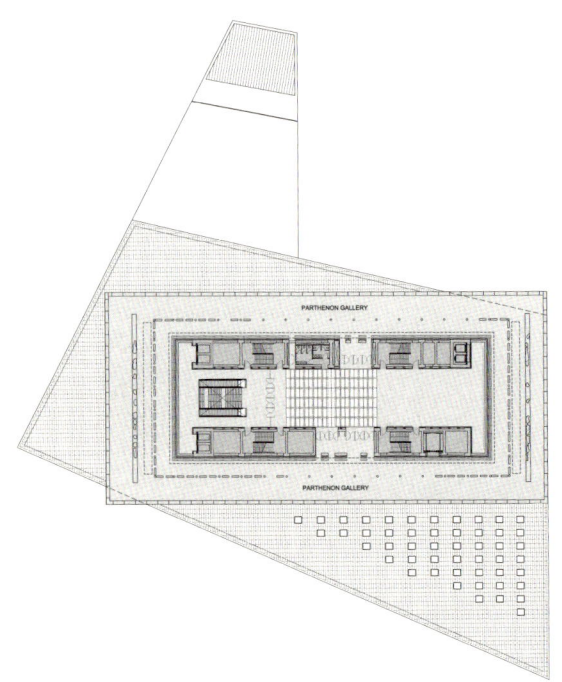

PARTHENON GALLERY

PARTHENON GALLERY

Floor plan of level +3

0 2,5 5   10   20

meters

N

Roof plan

TERRACE

0   2,5 5   10   20

meters

N

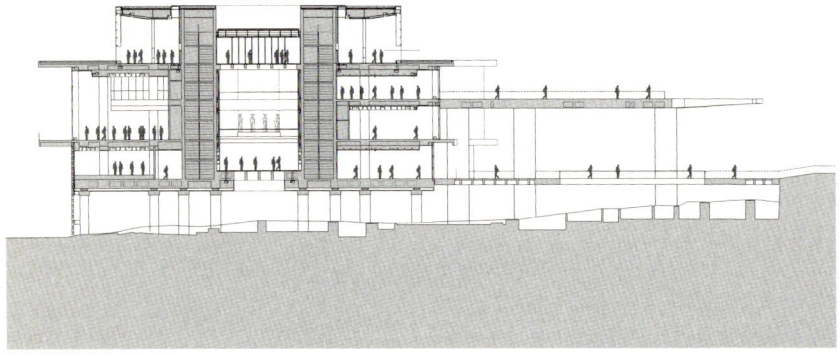

Transversal section

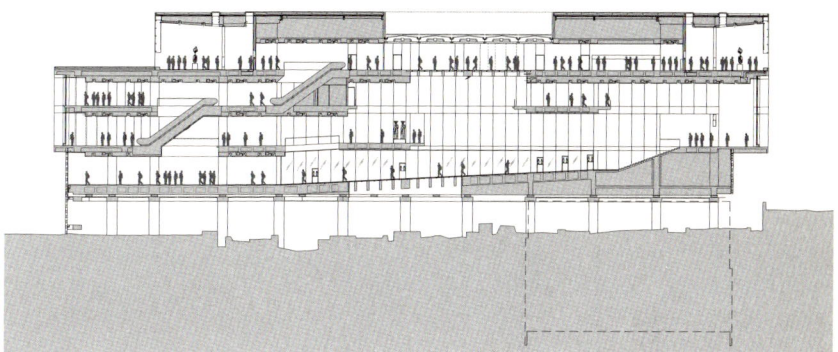

Longitudinal section

0   2,5 5   10   20

meters

N

The Acropolis Museum
under construction
Photos: Nikos Daniilidis

Sure. A folded wall or a sequence of layers is more related to new tools for planning (as computers) than to philosophical thinking. What role do you think new technologies play in the design process?

Just as the invention of the elevator changed the silhouette and the density of cities forever, new technologies of the building envelope have long changed the way we detail buildings. You do not need cornices or mullions anymore. Some computer software allows for spatial configurations that were hardly imaginable until just a few years ago.

And finally, with the construction of the building and the conditioning of the surrounding area completed, have you had any surprises? Does anything strike you as significantly different from your initial image?

Architecture is both concept and experience. You cannot replace the experience of your senses by a diagram. So seeing the building being built was an extraordinary moment. It confirmed the concept or, if we return to the theorem analogy, it was its own demonstration.

PHOTOGRAPHIC ESSAY

Peter Mauss

Exterior shots of the
Acropolis Museum
34-37

View of the surrounding
with the Parthenon
38-39

View of excavations
under the Museum
40-41

The Parthenon Gallery
42-43

The Parthenon Gallery, displaying
portions of the Parthenon Frieze
44

Interior of the building
with view of the Parthenon
45

The Archaic Gallery
46-51

Gallery of the Slopes
52-56

Hecatombedon Pediment
57

Statues from the Porch of the
Caryatids welcome visitors
58-59

Views to the excavations
under the Museum
60-63

Museum entrance at night
showing excavations
64-65

View of the Museum at dusk
66

The South Facade at night,
showing relationship of the
Parthenon Gallery to the Acropolis
67

Museum entrance at dusk
68-69

South Facade at night
70-71

The challenges of designing the new Acropolis Museum began with the responsibility of housing the most dramatic sculptures of Greek Antiquity. This collection of
objects shaped the program even before a site was chosen. The building's polemi-
cal location added further layers of responsibility to the design. Located at the foot
of the Acropolis, the site confronted us with sensitive archaeological excavations,
with the presence of the contemporary city of Athens and its street grid, and with
the Parthenon itself, one of the most influential buildings in Western civilization.
Combined with a hot climate in an earthquake region, these conditions moved us
to design a simple and precise museum with the mathematical and conceptual
clarity of ancient Greece.

We first articulated the building into a base, middle, and top, which are designed
around the specific needs of each part of the program. The base of the museum floats
on pilotis over the existing archaeological excavations, protecting and consecrating the
site with a network of columns placed in careful negotiation with experts so as not to
disturb the sensitive work. This level contains the entrance lobby as well as temporary
exhibition spaces, an auditorium, and all support facilities.

A glass ramp overlooking the archaeological excavations leads to the galleries in the
middle, in the form of a spectacular double-height room supported by tall columns.
This level accommodates displays from the Archaic period to the Roman Empire.

The top, which is made up of the rectangular Parthenon Gallery arranged around an
indoor court, has been rotated gently to orient the marbles of the frieze exactly as
they were at the Parthenon centuries ago. Its transparent enclosure provides ideal
light for sculpture in direct view to and from the Acropolis using the most contemporary glass technology to protect the gallery against excessive heat and light. This
new setting offers an unprecedented context for understanding the accomplishments
of the Acropolis complex. One of the goals of the top gallery is to reunite the Parthenon Frieze, currently dispersed in several world museums.

The conditions animating exhibition spaces revolve around natural light. Not only
does the daylight in Athens differ from light in London, Berlin, or New York; light for
the exhibition of sculpture differs from the light involved in displaying paintings or
drawings. The new museum can be described as an environment of ambient natural

light, concerned with the presentation of sculptural objects within it, whose display changes throughout the course of the day.

A circulation route narrates a rich spatial experience from the city street into the historical world of the different periods of archaeological inquiry. The visitor's route through the museum forms a clear three-dimensional loop, affording an architectural and historical promenade that extends from the archaeological excavations, visible through a glass floor in the entrance gallery, to the Parthenon Frieze in a gallery with views over the city, and back down through the Roman period. Movement in and through time is an important aspect of architecture—and of this museum in particular. With more than 10,000 visitors expected daily, the movement sequence through the museum artifacts is designed to be of the utmost clarity.

Materials have been selected for simplicity and sobriety: glass, concrete, and marble are the materials of choice. Perfectly transparent glass gently filters the light through a silkscreen-shading process. Concrete (both precast and cast-in-place) provides the main building structure and is the background for most of the artwork. Marble marks the floor: black for circulation, light beige for the galleries. Construction progressed according to exacting standards so that the building will age gracefully, despite the heavy traffic of this international travel destination.

Bernard Tschumi
Principal
Bernard Tschumi Architects

Conception

Designed along sober horizontal lines of extreme simplicity, the museum is intentionally not a monument itself. Instead, it is designed to focus the visitor's attention on the remarkable artworks on display. The plan translates the requirements of the program into architecture with supreme clarity.

Lighting: The collections consist in the main of sculptures, most of which were architectural elements that originally decorated the monuments of the Acropolis. As a result, the museum in which they are displayed is an environment bathed in ambient natural lighting. The use of various types of glass allows the light to spread around the upper Parthenon Gallery and through the skylights in the galleries of works dating from the Archaic period and to penetrate into the core of the building, coming gently to rest on the archaeological ruins situated in the lower level.

Circulation: The collections are arranged in chronological order from prehistoric times to the Late Roman era but reach their apogee (literally and architecturally) in the Parthenon Frieze. The route followed by visitors thus forms a clear three-dimensional loop. From the entrance lobby, the visitor walks along short ramp with the Gallery of the Slopes to a set of stairs leading to the Archaic period galleries, which are two floors high. From the Archaic Gallery, a pair of escalators lead up to the Parthenon Gallery before descending back down through the galleries of works from the Roman Empire, eventually coming out opposite the Acropolis itself.

The Building Layout: The museum consists of a lower, middle, and top level. Its shape was determined by the archaeological excavations underneath and by the orientation of the top level looking out toward the Parthenon.

The base level floats above the excavations on a hundred concrete pilotis. This level houses the entrance lobby, temporary exhibition rooms, storerooms, and museum restrooms.

The middle level (which is trapezoidal in floor plan) is a two-story-high space stretching ten meters up to the ceiling. It contains the galleries of works dating from the Archaic period to the Late Roman era. The mezzanine houses a bar and restaurant (with outdoor area, open to the public, looking out toward the Acropolis) and a multimedia space.

The top level contains the Parthenon Gallery, a rectangular space with glass walls and skylights; the Parthenon Gallery is almost seven meters high and has a surface area of about 2,000 square meters. It is rotated 23 degrees in relation to the rest of the building and is positioned along the same axis as the Acropolis. There, the core of the building that rises up through the various levels becomes the surface on which the marble sculptures of the Parthenon Frieze hang. This core allows the natural light to filter down on to the Caryatids on the level below.

Project
Acropolis Museum, Athens, Greece

Address
15 Dionysiou Areopagitou Street, Athens

Architects
Bernard Tschumi, Principal
Bernard Tschumi Architects, New York and Paris

Project Architect
Joel Rutten

Project Team
Adam Dayem, Aristotelis Dimitrakopoulos, Jane Kim, Eva Sopeoglou, Kim Starr, Anne Save de Beaurecueil, Jonathan Chace, Robert Holton, Valentin Bontjes van Beek, Liz Kim, Daniel Holguin, Kriti Siderakis, Michaela Metcalfe, Justin Moore, Joel Aviles, Georgia Papadavid, Allis Chee, Thomas Goodwill, Véronique Descharrières, Christina Devizzi

Associate Architects
ARSY Ltd., Athens
Michael Photiadis, Principal

Project Team
George Criparacos, Nikos Bakalbassis, Philippos Photiadis, Jaimie Peel, Niki Plevri, Maria Sarafidou, Makis Grivas, Elena Voutsina, Manolis Economou, Anastassia Gianou, Miltiadis Lazaridis, Dimitris Kosmas

Planning
Architect announcement: September 2001
Laying of the first stone: September 2003
Building completed: September 2007
Limited public access to museum premises: January 2008
Opening: June 20, 2009

Surface area
Overall surface area: 21,000 square meters
Display space: 14,000 square meters

Building contractor
Aktor

Budget
€130 million (approx. $175 million)

Financing
The museum was co-financed by the Hellenic Republic and the European Regional Development Fund (ERDF).

Program
With a total surface area of 21,000 square meters, more than 14,000 of which are given over to exhibition space, and benefiting from a vast array of modern facilities for visitors, the new Acropolis Museum will provide detailed insights into life on the Acropolis and its surroundings in Athens by bringing together the collections currently scattered around numerous institutions, among them the old Acropolis Museum (built in the nineteenth century and which had an exhibition space of under 1,500 square meters). The program includes a 200-seat auditorium, a café, a store, and a restaurant.

Consultants
Structure: ADK and Arup, New York
Fluids: MMB Study Group S.A. and Arup, New York
Engineering: Michanniki Geostatiki and Arup, New York
Lighting: Arup, London
Acoustics: Theodore Timagenis

SELECT BIBLIOGRAPHY

_ "Athens: Bernard Tschumi's Competition-Winning Scheme for the Acropolis Museum." *Architecture Today* (London), no. 125 (February 2002): 15.

_ "Athènes: Le nouveau museé de l'Acropole emmènage." *Archéologia* (Paris), no. 449 (November 2007): 4–5.

_ Beard, Mary. "Classical Comeback." *Royal Academy* (London), no. 98 (Spring 2008): 39.

_ Bernard Tschumi Architects, ed. *The New Acropolis Museum.* New York: Rizzoli International Publications, 2009.

_ Catsaros, Christophe. "Noveau Musée de l'Acropole, Athènes." *d'Architectures* (France), no. 170 (February 2008): 56–59.

_ Coen, Lorette. "Bernard Tschumi, Constructeur du movement." *PME Magazine/ Le Temps* (Geneva) Succès! Supplement (April 2008): 4–11.

_ Damiani, Giovanni, ed. *Bernard Tschumi.* Milan: Skira, 2003; London: Thames and Hudson, 2003. (Includes essays by K. Michael Hays and Giovanni Damiani and an interview with Marco De Michelis)

_ "De Vuelta a la Acropolis." *Pasajes* (Madrid), no. 36 (April 2002): 18.

_ Dillon, David. "Tschumi-Designed Acropolis Museum Opens." *Architectural Record* (New York) 197, no. 6 (June 2009).

_ Gage, Eleni. "New Acropolis Museum." *Travel+Leisure* (New York), November 2008.

_ Glancey, Jonathan. "Acropolis Now." *The Guardian* (London), 3 December 2007, p. 23.

_ Glover, Michael. "Olympic Effort." *ArtNews* (New York) 101, no. 3 (March 2002): 60.

_ Gonchar, Joann. "A Temple to Transparency Rises in Athens." *Architectural Record* (New York) 196, no. 6 (June 2007): 176–79.

_ Illia, Tony. "Commission for Acropolis Museum, Intended as Home for Elgin Marbles, Goes to Tschumi." *Architectural Record* (New York) 189, no.12 (December 2001): 28.

_ Kilston, Lyra. "Modern Ruins." *Modern Painters* (New York) 21, no. 5 (Summer 2009): 28–29.

_ Kostrenčić, Alan. "Light and Shadow." *ORIS* (Zagreb) 61 (2010): 20–35.

_ Lobell, Jarrett. "Acropolis Museum Back on Track and Wants the Parthenon Marbles to Come Home." *Archaeology* (New York) 57, no. 4 (July/August 2004): 10–12.

_ Morel, Guillaume. "L'Acropole s'offre un nouveau musée." *Connaissance Des Arts* (Paris), no. 674 (September 2009): 106–11.

_ "Neues Akropolismuseum." *StadtBauwelt* (Germany), no. 152 (December 2001): 9.

_ "New Acropolis Museum." *Bauwelt* (Berlin), no. 32–33 (August 2009): 13–39.

_ "New Acropolis Museum Athens." *Blueprint* (London), no. 260 (November 2007): 76–80.

_ "New Acropolis Museum, Athens, Greece." *IW Magazine* (Taiwan), no. 68 (July 2009): 52–59.

_ Ouroussoff, Nicolai. "Where Gods Yearn for Long-Lost Treasures." *New York Times* (New York), 21 October 2007, p. AR1, pp. 32–33.

_ Pearman, Hugh. "New Athens Museum Needs Parthenon Sculptures." *The Sunday Times* (London), 28 June 2009.

_ Rosenbaum, Lee. "Meeting of the Marbles?" *Art in America* (New York), no. 5 (May 2003): 41.

_ Ryan, Raymund. "Letter From America." *The Plan* (Milan), no. 036 (September 2009): 2–16.

_ Smith Macisaac, Heather. "One for the Ages: The New Acropolis Museum Debuts Soon." *Culture+Travel* (New York) 2, no. 1 (Winter 2007): 26–30.

_ Stephens, Suzanne. "New Acropolis Museum." *Architectural Record* (New York) 197, no. 10 (October 2009): 76–83.

_ "The New Acropolis Museum." *Concept* (Seoul), no. 110 (June 2008): 74–77.

_ "The New Acropolis Museum." *GA Document International* (Tokyo), no. 79 (April 2004): 64.

_ Timm, Tobias. "Antike im Glaskasten." *Die Zeit* (Hamburg), *KulturSommer* Supplement, April 2008.

_ Tschumi, Bernard. *Event-Cities 3: Concept vs. Context vs. Content.* Cambridge, Mass., and London: MIT Press, 2004.

_ *Tschumi on Architecture: Conversations with Enrique Walker.* New York: The Monacelli Press, 2006. (With Enrique Walker)

_ "Un cofre de crystal para las joyas de la Acrópolis." *GEO* (Madrid), no. 201 (October 2003): 14.

_ Wise, Michael. "Acropolis Now." *Architect Magazine* (Washington, D.C.) 98, no. 9 (September 2009): 48–51.